MUCIZE INSAN

Abhijit Naskar is the twenty-first century Neuroscientist whose contributions in Cognitive and Behavioral Neuroscience have helped the world tackle the issues of systemic racism, prejudice, hate, extremism, discrimination and biases more effectively. As an untiring advocate of mental health and universal acceptance, he became a beloved best-selling author all over the world with his very first book "The Art of Neuroscience in Everything". With his pioneering ventures into the Neuropsychology of beliefs and biases, he has hugely contributed in the eradication of religious and cultural differences in our world, for which he is popularly hailed as the humanitarian scientist, who takes the human civilization in the path of sweet general harmony.

MUCIZE
INSAN

When The World
is Family

ABHIJIT NASKAR

Also by Abhijit Naskar

The Art of Neuroscience in Everything
Your Own Neuron: A Tour of Your Psychic Brain
The God Parasite: Revelation of Neuroscience
The Spirituality Engine
Love Sutra: The Neuroscientific Manual of Love
Homo: A Brief History of Consciousness
Neurosutra: The Abhijit Naskar Collection
Autobiography of God: Biopsy of A Cognitive Reality
Biopsy of Religions: Neuroanalysis towards Universal
Tolerance
Prescription: Treating India's Soul
What is Mind?
In Search of Divinity: Journey to The Kingdom of Conscience
Love, God & Neurons: Memoir of a scientist who found
himself by getting lost
The Islamophobic Civilization: Voyage of Acceptance
Neurons of Jesus: Mind of A Teacher, Spouse & Thinker
Neurons, Oxygen & Nanak
The Education Decree
Principia Humanitas
The Krishna Cancer
Rowdy Buddha: The First Sapiens
We Are All Black: A Treatise on Racism
The Bengal Tigress: A Treatise on Gender Equality
Either Civilized or Phobic: A Treatise on Homosexuality
Wise Mating: A Treatise on Monogamy
Illusion of Religion: A Treatise on Religious
Fundamentalism
The Film Testament
Human Making is Our Mission: A Treatise on Parenting
I Am The Thread: My Mission
7 Billion Gods: Humans Above All
Lord is My Sheep: Gospel of Human
Morality Absolute
A Push in Perception
Let The Poor Be Your God
Conscience over Nonsense
Saint of The Sapiens
Time to Save Medicine
Fabric of Humanity
Build Bridges not Walls: In the name of Americana
The Constitution of The United Peoples of Earth

Lives to Serve Before I Sleep
When Humans Unite: Making A World Without Borders
All For Acceptance
Monk Meets World
Mission Reality
Citizens of Peace: Beyond The Savagery of Sovereignty
Operation Justice: To Make A Society That Needs No Law
See No Gender
The Gospel of Technology
Every Generation Needs Caretakers: The Gospel of
Patriotism
Aşkanjali: The Sufi Sermon
Mad About Humans: World Maker's Almanac
Revolution Indomable
When Call The People: My World My Responsibility
No Foreigner Only Family
Hurricane Humans: Give me accountability, I'll give you
peace
Ain't Enough to Look Human
Servitude is Sanctitude
Time To End Democracy: The Meritocratic Manifesto
I Vicdansaadet Speaking: No Rest Till The World is Lifted
Boldly Comes Justice: Sentient not Silent
Good Scientist: When Science and Service Combine
Sleepless for Society
Neden Türk: The Gospel of Secularism
Martyr Meets World: To Solve The Hard Problem of
Inhumanity
The Shape of A Human: Our America Their America
When Veins Ignite: Either Integration or Degradation
Heart Force One: Need No Gun to Defend Society
Solo Standing on Guard: Life Before Law
Generation Corazon: Nationalism is Terrorism

DEDICATION

This book is dedicated to my sisters and brothers of Palestine. I won't rest till I see you free.

CONTENTS

1. You Are The Road

Nobody is born with a brain full of knowledge and wisdom. All you can be born with is an intention for learning. When you have the intention you can gather knowledge and the more you practice that knowledge the more wise you become. So a peaceful and inclusive world is not really a matter of knowledge or intellect, it is a matter of intention. How much do you want it - that is the question!

Contrary to wisdom, all brains are born with instincts. And in the absence of the intention for an inclusive society those instincts facilitate a savage mind full with prejudices. Prejudice is the default mode of thinking of every animal, not excluding the human, unless you the human actually practice civilized thought.

Civilization is like a muscle of the mind, the more you practice it, the stronger it gets, and the stronger it gets, the more powerful it becomes against the innate tendencies of primitiveness. You see, space is not the final frontier, humanity is, the full manifestation of humanity, above the influence of biases, for it is much easier to conquer outer space than inner space.

At this point, terraforming a planet (transforming a planet to sustain life) is luxury, whereas reforming our own society is necessity, yet most of humanity is super excited about terraforming Mars than they are about reforming their homeworld.

In fact, I've come across many such people who boast about the scientific and technological advancements of humankind and yet when it comes to matters of justice and equality, they brush 'em off as unfriendly topics of politics. And with such callousness on the part of the everyday, ordinary citizens (which include everyone), no politician or policy can enforce order and progress in society.

I shall call you human the day your fascination for external advancement turns dull in front of your fascination for society, in front of your responsibleness for society (responsibility doesn't quite sound right). The worth of a person lies in their responsibleness for society, not in their economic or intellectual caliber. Responsibleness is the test of humanness, unselfishness is the test of humanness.

Let me put it to you simply. To live for soil and society is real humanity, it is real religion, it is real advancement. Think of the most beautiful word in any language, and it is bound to be a reflection of humanity one way or another. Remember, all roads lead to people, to humankind. And here is the interesting part. You are the road yourself.

6

2.   We Are Yet to Discover Life

There is no predestined course of action for the human being, for you are the destiny personified. Whatever you want your destiny to be, it is all in your hands - whatever you want the destiny of your society to be, it is all in your hands. The real question is, are you going to wash off that responsibility by dumping it on the politicians? If you do, then that's it, your worth as a human turns null.

Let me give you a few facts. We have discovered a lot as a species, we've discovered science, we've discovered philosophy, we've discovered religion, we've discovered democracy, but we are yet to discover life in our existence. And the day you realize your responsibility for society, you'll automatically discover that life as well. Responsibility is sanity, complacency is insanity.

We are the explorers of upliftment. Whatever upliftment there has been, it has been caused by human intervention - whatever upliftment there is to come, 'tis to be caused by human intervention, by our own sweat and blood. You see, questioning the government is easy, what takes character is to be the solution.

There are mostly two types of people in the world, those who adjust with every single inhumanity in society, and those who question and blame the government for all the inhumanities in society. But then, there are those rare few lionhearted characters who stand up to each inhumanity as the solution without passing the parcel of responsibility onto someone else. And these rare few individuals are the only true humans of planet earth, rest are mere mockery of human existence.

Blaming the government is easy, even a five year old child can do that, taking responsibility for what the government is responsible for, is the real sign of character. So, before you blame the government for something, ask yourself, do you have any solution to the problem you are mad about or do you at least have an idea on how to come up with a solution? If you do, then forget the government, and work on your individual capacity to put that solution to use, however you can.

3. Change Requires Character

Though you may assume the government to be high and mighty, the fact of the matter is, in the current prehistoric form of democracy government is mostly made up of people who are no more expert in anything than the regular civilians are. So, given that you are prepared to learn, you as a responsible civilian are capable of more change than a hundred boneheaded politicians. Change requires character, not politics.

And yes, here I am indeed generalizing politicians, (while of course confirming that there's always exception). You know why I am generalizing - because politics is the only dominant field in society that requires no credentials or qualifications whatsoever – all it requires is charm.

You want to be a doctor, you must go through years of education and training. You want to be a pilot, you must go through years of education and training. You want to be a cop, you must go through years of education and training. No matter what you want to be in society, you must go through years of rigorous education and training, except if you want to be a politician. You want to be a politician, all you gotta do is charm the people with your charisma, no matter your character or qualifications.

And when such a field without any backbone and foundation tends to be the primary driver of a society, then it is no civilized society to begin with. It is like having a world where sickness is treated by random people without any medical training. Hence, it is more reason, and rather imperative for the civilians to be responsible.

If a doctor screws up, they lose their license, if a lawyer screws up, they are disbarred, if a cop screws up, they end up in jail (it may be difficult, but not impossible), but if a politician screws up or takes advantage of their position, which is in fact accepted as the norm, then it is more likely for them to walk free than to be held accountable, cause they are the very authority of all law, as presumed by the people - the people who couldn't tell a chimpanzee from a gorilla if they are charming enough. You see, a characterless politician is the reflection of a characterless citizenry.

4. Sonnet of Citizens

Sonnet of Citizens

What can the politicians do,
Unless the people allow it!
What can the government do,
Unless the people permit it!
All corruption is born of people,
Not of politics and bureaucracy.
Corrupt politicians are only symptom,
Real disease is populist democracy.
Politics is civilized when people are civilized,
But what we have is politics of blame.
Denounce blaming and take responsibility,
Then only will your children live without shame.
Your indifference fuels all political histrionics.
Build your character and there'll be no politics.

5. Citizens Are The Disease, Not Politicians

Corrupt politicians are not the disease, they are the symptom, the real disease are the citizens who prefer indifference over humanity. So, if the society is to turn civilized, the people must be civilized first, that is, they must turn accountable first and learn to distinguish character beyond the smokescreen of lies.

And only a being of character can distinguish character in another person. So people must build their own character first. Each of us is to build our character, only then there is gonna be hope for true upliftment in society - and more importantly, only then there'll be humanity in the human society.

I don't expect much from the politicians, all my dreams of a civilized, united, occupation-free, dictatorship-free world are predicated on the actions of the everyday, responsible individuals of society. No matter your status, no matter your salary, all that is necessary is that you have accountability. An accountable human is a model human, rest are lesser replicas.

If someone stands up fortified with my ideas to enact reform in society, they are to do so because they are a person of character, not because they are a person of politics. You may choose politics as the means, as you may choose any other field as the means - the means is irrelevant, for your primary objective must always be the upliftment of the people.

For example, I am a scientist, but my objective is not the advancement of science (there are already plenty scientists for that purpose), my objective is to use science for the advancement of society, mental advancement to be precise. It is the upliftment of the people that counts, how you do it, that's up to you.

However, I want some of you to indeed be actively involved in politics as a hardcore politician, if you feel inclined in that direction, because if you keep letting those greedy fools without any vision for a united earth run the society, our world will never be emancipated from human rights violations, such as in Palestine or Kashmir – it will never be free from inter-nation conflicts. So, if you feel you can do it from within politics, then dive in lock, stock and barrel.

The world needs young, accountable and unorthodox politicians with the revolutionary vision of a unified planet, who are never afraid to correct their mistakes and grow according to the need of the time, rather than prehistoric buffoons with ideas and beliefs from the stone-age. Be energetic, be bold, be revolutionary.

If boneheads can wreak such havoc in society when they gain political power, imagine what a real human being of character could accomplish with such power! Play smart and with the benefit of the people in heart, treat politics like you'd treat any other potential tool. Remember, reform is alive through you, whether you bring it by means of politics or science or any other.

6. **Sonnet of Palestine**

Sonnet of Palestine

I don't want to wage a war,
All I want is to raise a family.
I don't want your empty pity,
All I seek is a little humanity.
To call genocide as self-defense,
May be textbook diplomacy.
Killing innocents to keep control,
Is an act of terrorist hypocrisy.
Brokers may bring ceasefire,
But they can never give us liberty.
All they do is arrange assemblies,
While we suffer through the century.
So I say to you o people in luxury,
Look at us and you'll know your fallacy.

7. **Sonnet of Kashmir**

Sonnet of Kashmir

Mindless nationalists of India shout,
India is the greatest nation.
Yet atrocities done in their backyard,
Make them a symbol of degradation.
Most Indians have no idea,
How it is to live under occupation.
Yet when it comes to the land of Kashmir,
They won't make any concession.
How can you reason with a deluded bunch,
Who value sovereignty over people!
They have their comfort and luxuries,
Who cares if we lack even life's essential!
Where land is more precious than life,
There lives no human but termite.

8.   Memorial Day Sonnet

Memorial Day Sonnet

We don't want your celebration,
We don't want you to honor us.
All we want is for you to grow up,
And end all tribalism that kills us.
A thousand holidays can't bring us back,
Nor can they wipe the tears of our spouses.
How will you console our children,
How will you comfort our broken parents!
Enough with your flowers and rituals,
Enough with your crocodile care!
If you have an iota of humanity,
Step up and make all divides disappear.
Yet if you still want to live life as tribal,
Rest assured we'll give ours with a smile.

9. Accountable Unorthodoxy is The Way

Reform is not a purpose in life, reform is life itself. Reform is not a destination, reform is the road itself. Reform is revolution, reform is rejuvenation, reform is salvation, reform is civilization. And in reform, there is no room for sectarianism, in reform there is no room for selfishness, in reform there is no room for separation between self and society.

Only the selfless can manifest humanity. Only those who want nothing for themselves are the true conquerors of the world - they are the true conquerors of time. Time forgets the selfish, but never the selfless. Sacrifice brings you eternal life, selfishness brings you eternal damnation. The course of sacrifice is the course of truth, for the course of sacrifice is the course of ascension.

The course of selfishness on the other hand is the course of prehistoric times. We cannot still keep walking on such primitive course while calling ourselves civilized. Prehistoric behavior belongs in prehistoric times. Prehistoric orthodoxy belongs in prehistoric times. You see, lifeless orthodoxy won't solve anything, accountable unorthodoxy will.

Here unorthodoxy is not to be confused with recklessness or rebelliousness. That's why I added accountable in front of it. Rebelling just for the sake of rebelling, accomplishes nothing. Here the focus is on being accountable, not on the act of rebellion. When your accountability makes you stand up to the uncivilized norms of society, that accountability may be deemed as rebellion, but in your mind, you are simply doing what's civilized.

You are not rebelling, because you think 'society says this, so let's do the opposite', for such would only be an act of yet another form of savagery. Do what is right, not for the sake of rebellion, but for the sake of civilization. Civilization starts with you, it starts with accountability. Accountability makes way for reason, accountability makes way for assimilation.

The conservatives often whine about how all walks of society have been taken over by progressives and liberals. The reality is, no walk of society is taken over by progressives and liberals - it's just that, reason and assimilation have slowly but surely been redeeming the world from the prehistoric clutches of prejudice, ignorance and narrowness.

And you see, the only reason conservatives still have a voice in a budding world of reason and inclusion is because it is a world of acceptance, not a world of exclusion and narrowness - had it been a world run by those very conservatives, all voice of reason would've been silenced by prehistoric legislative means, like they continue to be in Turkey, India, France and so on. It is this simple, in a civilized world even bigots have a voice, but in a bigoted world, the only place where you can find reason and inclusion is prison.

42

43

10. Dumb People with Smart Phones

44

Brain balance is more important than bank balance. Brain balance doesn't mean mere intellect, brain balance means having a sound mind and well-built character. And most of humanity seems to run low on sound mind and character. Though we may look fancy on the outside with our modern clothes and superficial gadgets, in our heart, we are still prehistoric savages.

Furthermore, those very gadgets sustain our savagery, by conditioning us to remain discontent all our life. For example, person wearing an apple watch is like a dog with an electric collar - every time the dog does something wrong it receives a high voltage shock, thus conditioning it to walk the line - likewise a person receives a vibration every few minutes that keep them craving for more attention all hours of the day.

Then these tech giants exploit their discontent further by selling them more products and subscriptions of meditation lessons, just like the tradesmen of traditional methods do. It's enough already. Enough meditation, it's time for revolution - for the love of people, for the rights of people, for humanity.

Want to be content and find happiness - then you must discard all habits that facilitate self-obsession. If you cared for the society as your own family, you'd have neither the time nor the need for meditation. But in today's world, meditation is yet another way to butter the vanity of a pompous population already teeming with self-obsession, just like those fancy gadgets do that keep popping up every day.

For example, apple watch, that is, smartwatch is a great technology, but it is yet to be utilized for actually the benefit of humankind, as opposed to AirPods and AirTag, which can serve distinct positive purposes in life without disrupting the wellbeing of the mind. At some point smartwatch and smartphone will become one, and then perhaps the existence of smartwatch will make sense, but until then every smartwatch is just a vain accessory for your smartphone that you are made to believe that you need.

However, here what I must also point out is, like in any other field of advancement, you cannot magically skip steps, which means, we cannot jump from smartphone in our pockets to smartphone on our wrists, without first developing the smartwatch as sort of a bridge between the two. But the attention of a company must be on the welfare of its consumers, not on draining their wallets.

11. When Tech Serves Society

50

Every technology has potential, but to realize that potential and use it for good, we must look beyond the bounds of profit margin. Facebook couldn't, hence it is bound to perish and become the next orkut, sooner than you imagine. It is this simple, purpose driven technology will continue to flourish, whereas profit driven technology will either perish or destroy the world.

Let's take climate change for example. Carbon emission from regular cars is a fundamental ingredient that has been destabilizing earth's climate. Technology caused this catastrophe, but now that we know about it, we can use the same technology to stop it - electric vehicle powered by renewable energy being one such technology.

Also, here one thing I must mention - for electric vehicles to make an impact on climate change, they must be powered by renewable energy sources, otherwise, the powerplants producing the electricity to power the vehicles would end up dumping more greenhouse gas into the atmosphere than we are able to reduce by replacing regular vehicles with electric ones.

Now comes the economic aspect of the matter. If we are to make significant strides in climate action through electric vehicles, then producing them as a class statement for the rich won't do, they must be made affordable enough to be owned by the vast population of working classes. And I do not expect Tesla or Apple to make it happen, if it is achieved it is more likely to be done by some less popular yet more responsible firm.

Now here if somebody tries to defend Apple saying that Apple cares about the privacy of its users more than any other company, to them I say, Apple doesn't care about privacy, any more than Erdogan cares about secularism in Turkey. All it cares about is privacy for the privileged. Till this day, Apple hasn't intentionally made one single innovation to actually benefit the ordinary people of planet earth.

Now here one question that may rise in the minds of some, which in fact I was asked in a recent Discord interview, is, wouldn't it be better if we got rid of all technology altogether? To which I say, such notion is as biased as those that promote absolute domination of technology without any caution whatsoever.

So I repeat again, I am not anti-technology, for as a teenager I was obsessed with building various tech. Technology is not necessarily evil, we just need to have a firm grasp of right and composed use of technology in life and society. Healthy and humane use of technology lies beyond the glory and gloom of innovation.

54

12. Sonnet of Technology

Sonnet of Technology

Technology is not good or bad,
For it knows no ethics and principles.
The prime directive of all gadgets,
Is to obey algorithm without scruples.
The problem is not technology,
Nor is it the capitalist tendency.
The real disease is human recklessness,
Which is rampant in modern society.
Your phone is not ruining your peace,
You yourself are doing it all.
A society oblivious to moderation,
In time causes its own downfall.
Power is power only when used with caution,
If used wildly all power is poison.

13. Into The Heart of Technology

The reason you are able to read me, while I am still alive and young, is by the grace of technology. Had there been no technology, by the time you get to learn about my work, I'd have been long dead, particularly when I do not come from either a wealthy or an academic family.

That is the reason, whatever you may say about technology, I cannot dis it in right mind. But I cannot turn a blind eye to its harms either. So I say, you don't need to renounce technology to live a healthy and happy life, you just need to reorganize its purpose in your life. Let me put it in simpler terms. It is okay to own a technology, what is not okay is to be owned by technology.

It is high time we place welfare of the people at the heart of all technology. People over profit - that's the motto for the world of innovation. Facebook practices the absolute opposite of this motto, because of which I stopped using my personal facebook profile over a year back.

And one more thing - if you are worried about privacy, then let me be very clear on the matter - there is no company in the world that can provide absolute online privacy to its users, no matter how much they showcase privacy as one of their prime features. If you strictly want something not to get on the internet, do not keep it on your phone. Internet and privacy are anti-thesis of each other. No device connected to the internet is unhackable, whether it's android, windows or iOS. Know this and then use the internet.

Here I repeat, I am neither anti nor pro anything, I just value life too much to be either swayed by the charm of technology or be disheartened by the gloom of technology. Technology is one of the greatest accomplishments of the human species, that holds unimaginable potential, but like all great power, it can be used for either good or bad. The decision lies in our hands - to be precise, the right utilization of technology is predicated on our accountability. Let me put it into perspective. A hundred falcon rockets and a hundred teslas can be sacrificed to save one human life, but no human is to be exploited for the advancement of all the rockets and all the cars in the world.

14. Character Over Privacy

64

Now let's look into another aspect of privacy. If you are not doing anything wrong, that is, immoral, then why do you need to be bothered with privacy! If you are behaving as a healthy and conscientious human being, then why do you need to worry about privacy! What are you doing that is so shameful that it must be kept a secret?

Let me elaborate with a few examples. If you are in a relationship and you are having an intimate conversation with your partner on text or call, isn't it something normal for two people in relationship! If you are sending each other nudes, what is so wrong about it that you need to be ashamed of it! Yes it may be awkward if those pics get public, but on the off chance that they do get public, why should you regret it! You didn't do anything wrong, so why should you be ashamed of it!

Having cleared that, because such pics and texts are better kept private, you ought to be cautious while sharing them and that too not over some generic and popular app such as messenger or whatsapp. When I was in a relationship, I used Signal for private conversations. Though there is no such thing as absolute privacy on the internet, some apps are less unsafe than others.

However, never forget, when you live as a conscientious human being, there is nothing for you to be ashamed of. It's only the shallow and the hypocrites who are obsessed with privacy, because they have something to hide. Focus on your character and you won't need to worry about privacy. A well-built character is the epitome of righteousness, hence, above the petty insecurities and rigidities of society.

15. Common Sense Over Conspiracy

68

The unfortunate reality is, the lifeblood of society is not character but rigidity. And it infects every newborn that sees the light of day. Thus we have a world full of creatures that care more about normal behavior than righteous behavior. Character brings real liberation of mind and it is when the mind is free from rigidity and insecurity can it set in motion righteous human behavior. Righteousness, principles, ethics, morality, all these are born of character. To the being of character, all these come naturally, rest only try to find them in etiquettes, mindfulness classes and self-help books.

Then there are those who, quite unbeknownst to themselves are driven subconsciously to cover up their insecurities with thoughts of self-victimization, where they believe the whole world is out to get them, particularly societal institutions, such as the government, media, scientific and medical experts and so on. Then they do a bit of googling and quite naturally their mind cherry-picks the data that strengthen their belief further, and set out on a crusade against all institutions and expertise of society, without actually having a clue as to the real problems of the world, just like militant nationalists and religious fundamentalists live their life as a living crusade against all possibilities of harmony, inclusion and global unification of humankind.

You see, having the data is not the same as having the expertise to look through the data - if it were, everybody with a smartphone would be a doctor or a scientist. Let me put it another way. It is the prerogative of the masses to pick on the shortcomings of science, but had it not been for that very science, those very masses would still be living in the jungle and dying early from easily treatable ailments. Science is not perfect, but it is by far our most powerful weapon against the atrocities of nature as well as our most effective tool in the course of development.

71

16. Sonnet of Conspiracy

Sonnet of Conspiracy

Perhaps there's a monster under the bed,
Perhaps there's a boogeyman in the closet.
Perhaps they're sterilizing kids with vaccine,
Perhaps they're controlling all with a radio set.
Yes our science is well advanced,
But not advanced enough to control minds.
Besides mind-control needs no fancy tech,
When people are run by smartphone chimes.
Tales like these are good for entertainment,
Amongst a bunch of kindergarteners.
But being adult requires the use of reason,
Without submitting to prehistoric fears.
Treating insecurities with common sense,
Anyone can manifest civilized sentience.

17. The Vaccine Sonnet

76

The Vaccine Sonnet

Listen to the experts,
Listen to Fauci.
Grow up you big sissy,
Enough with the ouchie!
I got the vaccine,
Trust me it's safe.
Every scientist will confirm,
Listen to reason not hearsay.
Vaccines produce immunity,
Masks prevent the spread.
If you follow some simple steps,
You'll prevent someone's death.
Freedom without reason is savagery.
During pandemic accountability is key.

.

18. La Vacuna Soneto

La Vacuna Soneto

Escuche a los expertos,
Escuche a la ciencia.
¡Madura flojo inmaduro,
Ten algo de valentía!
Me puse la vacuna,
Créame es seguro.
Cada sientifico lo confirmará,
Escucha a la razón, no al chismorreo.
Las vacunas producen inmunidad,
Las mascarillas previenen la propagación.
Si sigues unos simples pasos,
Prevendras la muerte de alguien.
La libertad sin razón es un salvajismo.
En crisis la responsabilidad es imperativo.

19. Growth is Power

84

Science becomes more powerful each day, because it recognizes that it is not perfect and continues to work on those imperfections ceaselessly. The same holds true for the individual. One who recognizes their shortcomings and never stops working on them, is bound to keep growing. And such an ever-growing individual is the true being of character.

And a being of character recognizes the good as well as the bad in every aspect of society, then steps up to strengthen the good while eliminating the bad, with thoughts, emotions and actions. You see, nobody is out to get you. And more importantly, why would they even care!

Feed your character with reason and warmth, so that you learn to recognize and realize the real troubles that haunt our human society. If you don't - if you continue to let your prejudice and ignorance overwhelm you with conspiracies to give you a sense of subconscious comfort against your powerlessness, then I'm afraid, you'll spend your precious life like a grumpy old, superstitious nut, who has nothing good to offer this world, so all they do is whine about how they are being victimized by the system.

All conspiracy theories are the product of the subconscious attempt of an ignorant yet creative mind to counteract the fear of the unknown with tales of fantasy. But here's the thing - making up tales of fantasy or fortune from the bottom of a tea cup may make good conversation piece, but they don't lift our society one inch. Reason, reason and reason - that's the only antidote to superstition, prejudice and conspiracies - but for reason to work, you must have the desire to grow, even if it means going against your most precious and traditional beliefs.

All systems of society are flawed - they are flawed not because they are made to exploit people, they are flawed because they are made by humans. Now if a bunch of greedy, egotistical maniacs abuses those flaws to exploit others, that's not the fault of the system. So grow up and stop whining - come up with a solution, instead of being the problem.

Remember, the miracle human doesn't conjure wine out of water, they conjure real, practical solutions to the problems of our society out of their blood and sweat. When you annihilate the self in the upliftment of society, that's real miracle, all else are mere clever trickery.

20. Sonnet of Traditions

Sonnet of Traditions

Society must shed its dead traditions,
Like one sheds dead skin.
Anything that lives must evolve,
For stagnation is death's twin.
The difference between life and death,
Lies in the desire for evolution.
Fancy rags on a prehistoric mind,
Makes way for a horrific extinction.
Other animals lack brain power,
To overcome shortcomings and be better.
But the jelly inside the human skull,
Can take us on an endless adventure.
All that is old is not necessarily gold.
Accepting yesterday's good move ahead bold.

21. Sonnet of Stagnation

Sonnet of Stagnation

Stagnated water breeds disease,
When in motion it breathes life.
Stagnated mind breeds segregation,
When in motion it breaks divide.
Stagnated air breeds pollution,
When in motion it brings rejuvenation.
Stagnated ideas breed prejudice,
When in motion they bring illumination.
We are not a species, we are a family,
A stagnated psyche cannot feel its delight.
Open your eyes from your rigid sleep,
In your vision the world will unite.
All animals are bound to live in stagnation.
Only human neurons hold the capacity for expansion.

96

22. Who is Miracle Human
(The Sonnet)

98

Who is Miracle Human
(The Sonnet)

Who is the miracle human,
Can they turn water into wine?
Do they never run out of bread,
Can they turn cotton into golden twine?
None of this is actually miracle,
All these are stories of fantasy.
When ignorance was default thinking,
Magic defined a person's capacity.
Real miracle is an act of kindness,
Nothing is higher and more divine.
When you share happily your last bread,
That is holiness most genuine.
Rise and conquer all old prejudice and fantasy.
Stand firm and foster the miracle humanity.

23. Rebellion is Not Revolution

If it is the prerogative of the animals to stay silent, it is the duty of the humans to intervene. Be ready my soldiers of ascension, to rise and roar whenever the need arises. And remember, there's a time for being sentimental and there's a time for being scientific. Don't confuse the two. Recognize the need of the situation and act accordingly.

There is no 'one size fits all' solution to the myriad problems of the world. So, to solve each of these problems, you actually have to think for yourself, without the influence of tradition and opinions, those of your own as well as of others. But mark you, here I am not talking about some childish rebellion. Rebellion for the sake of rebellion is as futile as complacency.

Here what I am talking about is revolution. Revolution is not the same as rebellion, for all revolution involves rebellion, but not all rebellion is revolution. Revolution is driven by the purpose – the vision, of a better world, whereas rebellion is driven by sheer defiance of authority, just for the sake of proving oneself above the authority. Those who are really above all authority in their mind, have no desire to prove anything to anyone, it is only those who are actually seeking attention from the authority, that rebel against authority most dramatically.

One who is truly above authoritarian influence doesn't care about defiance or rebellion, all they care about in their heart is to be the living change that they want to see in their society. That's what a revolutionary looks like - that's what revolution looks like - no intentional defiance for the sake of defiance, just a whole lot of undeterred accountability in action.

Let me elaborate a bit further. In a society where stuffing yourself with booze is accepted as the norm, by keeping your boozing habits to bare minimum or refraining from it completely, you do not defy the norm of society, rather you are simply setting an example of healthy human behavior – you are showing the society how to be a society. And this is only possible when you have a well-built character, otherwise, you are bound to give in to the sick etiquettes of society in an attempt to be accepted by your peers. Remember, there is no such thing as peer-pressure, there's only lack of character.

Compromising your principles to adjust with the sick etiquettes of society doesn't make you any more civilized than those practicing such etiquettes. When the whole world is obsessed with its self-absorbed norms and rituals, if you can stand true to your conviction of humanity all on your own, then and then alone are you an actual, living, breathing, sentient human.

If this world is to turn from self-centric to community-centric, it can only start from the individual - it can only start from you. To understand the world you must start by saying, I know nothing. To serve the world you must start by saying, I am nothing. When the self disappears the world appears. Let me put this in practical terms with the example of nationality. When you wipe out your national allegiance, the whole world becomes your family, and then you start to see the real face of each nation, including their strongholds as well as their shortcomings.

In short, to awaken the human in you, you must first kill the tribal animal in you. Once you've done that, all reform will manifest on its own wherever you stand – and as a result all justice will manifest on its own in the society.

Social justice doesn't simply mean legal punishment for hate crime or reparations for slavery, social justice means a complete overhaul of our society from a self-centric, rigid and tribal community to a collectivity-centric, ever-growing, borderless community. And that can only happen with the overhaul of the individual psyche from tribal animal to a civilized human. World begins where the tribes end, civilization begins where tribalism ends.

24. We Are The Cause of Everything

There is a reason behind everything that happens to this world, and I am not talking about some imaginary, hocus focus, divine intervention sort for reason, but reason as in cause, involving everyday, ordinary, human action – just regular people living their life, driven by instincts and social norms that are also born mostly of instincts, without ever trying to rise above those instincts as a living, breathing, thinking life-form.

Every single habit or ritual of the so-called modern human, is a manifestation of primeval instincts, which are there since time immemorial to ensure one thing and one thing alone - preservation of the self. In short, if we dig deep into the habits, rituals and norms of the so-called civilized human, we'd find the plain, ordinary, uncivilized drive for selfishness.

And so long as selfishness drives the psyche of the individual, it'll drive the psyche of the world, and so long as selfishness drives the world, all systems born of such world is bound to facilitate narrowness and rigidity, rather than expansion and growth - be it the system of law and order, be it the system of science and technology, be it the system of faith or any other.

I've always lived a life of faith, but not the faith of the scripture, but that of selflessness. You see, there is no such thing as a holy book, there's only holy people. Individual becomes holy when they step across the self, or to put it simply without resorting to corrupted-beyond-repair terms like holy and religious - a creature becomes human when they step across the self to genuinely benefit another person.

And to create such nonsectarian beings is the mission of my life - beings who would be civilization incarnate - beings who won't be some higher race, but won't hesitate going down to the deepest pit of desolation to lift others up - beings whose very lifeblood would be service - whose nerves would be made of thunderbolts and heart made of honey.

Mark my words, I will be gone, but my ideas will continue to create hundreds of Subhas Chandra Boses and Martin Luther Kings in every neighborhood of this world, from the alleys of New York to the streets of Nairobi, from the beaches of Miami to the banks of

Kanyakumari, from the sidewalks of Ankara to
the foothills of Alaska.

25. No Excuses

114

Sleeping sound won't do, resting calm won't do - throw all security, all pleasures (may spare the little ones), all desires overboard - and envision in front of your eyes one goal, one dream, one mission - the mission of an elevated society - elevated from sectarianism into universalism - from the darkness of prejudice into the light of growth and learning - from the puddles of argumentation and arrogance into the ocean of assimilation and humility.

And don't let no brokenness keep you from the realization of your dream. Remember, our brokenness is our greatest strength. I've been broken all my life, for my life is one on the spectrum with OCD to make things worse. But have you ever heard me whine about my brokenness - no – never! For no matter how broken you are, till you give in to your brokenness, it can never break you. Embrace your brokenness, be it metaphorical or clinical, and it'll amplify your determination as well as your capacities beyond your wildest imagination.

No excuses, no whining - only an undeterred vision of a goal, such an undeterred vision that keeps you awake at night - that doesn't let you feel the taste of food - this my would-be patriot is my watchword for you. You are inferior to no one, you are superior to no one - you are the miracle human, who'll show the world what it means to be human, not by looking down on others, but by lifting them up while placing yourself beneath their feet.

You cannot lift the society by living on a pedestal, you must come down amidst the people. If your intellect separates you from the people, it's worthless intellect - if your philosophy separates you from the people, it's worthless philosophy - if your science separates you from the people, it's worthless science. Everything civilized that exists, must exist as the unifier of people, or else it has no role in civilized society.

You must unfold your heart to unfold civilization, for the unfolding of your heart is the unfolding of civilization. Arrogance won't do, pride won't do, recklessness won't do, self-aggrandizing won't do - accountability, accountability, accountability, - absolute, incorruptible accountability, that's what's needed. And this is only possible for a being of character.

A well-built character is heard around the world, even if it comes from the remotest of places, whereas a loudmouth without character isn't even heard two feet across no matter how much they shout. It's not the volume of your voice that matters, it's the content. Words of character can be heard light-years away, even if they are whispered. In fact, I wouldn't be surprised if some advanced life-form in some distant galaxy is browsing on their highly advanced internet at this very moment studying the works of humans with character. And the sign of a well-built character is expansion.

26. I Expand, Therefore I Am

Let everyone hear it, I expand, therefore I am. You see, 'I think, therefore I am', does not work anymore. It might have worked back in the days, when humankind was taking baby steps in their intellectual endeavors. But today, it ain't enough to simply think, you know why - because even the animals think to some extent. Therefore, thinking isn't enough, what matters is that our thinking is guided by a genuine desire for universality - a desire for collective good, and not merely by a primitive drive for self-centricity.

When universality engulfs your whole being, nothing, I repeat, nothing can stop humankind to actually become human. Remember, this is the great fact of civilized life, universality is civilization, exclusivity is dehydration. Etch this principle in your head and work towards it by any means that appeals to your heart.

Come what may, never stop working. When others praise you, keep a smile on your face, when others ridicule you, still keep a smile on your face. You are a sun my friend, the more you give, the brighter you shine. Come on to the practical field of world building and work ceaselessly with the last iota of strength.

It is this simple, either you are stir-crazy for reform or you are crazy complacent and calling the doers crazy. Reform requires unselfishness, for what is unselfish is also civilized. I know only one truth, unselfishness, all else are memories of a primitive past. Never yield to selfishness, the animals do, and look at how they live. If a human can't be unselfish, what's the point in being a human!

27. I Expand, Therefore I Am
(The Sonnet)

I Expand, Therefore I Am
(The Sonnet)

I expand, therefore I am,
Thought is no measure of sapiens.
Even a dog can think what's best for it,
Such selfishness is no existence.
Expansion makes the human,
Inclusion strengthens life.
Diversity beautifies society,
There is no room for divide.
Sanity lies in unselfishness,
Selfishness is inhumanity.
When all world becomes one family,
That my friend is true community.
Let us be vast and breathe in the world.
Let us show all, the blue dot is no less bold.

127

28. Lovenut

The power of a paradigm comes from the consent of people. If the people wake up from their prehistoric sleep of selfishness, then no selfish paradigm can survive in this world to begin with. So, if someone shouts that the society is selfish, they have only themselves to blame. Till the individual stops throwing dirt on others and takes the responsibility of their society upon their own shoulders, nothing is going to change. You want change - be unselfish first.

Unselfishness is the lifeblood of every modern renaissance. You have to become a lovenut for society, for the society to turn civilized. Great civilization requires great sacrifice. And great civilization is established through a thousand stumbles. Stumble - time after time, but always, I repeat, always - get back up and start working again.

In this hell of a society, only sign of heaven is an unselfish heart. So I say it to you simply - heaven is not a place, it's a person, it's you when you are unselfish. Progress is not a destination, it's a journey of an unselfish heart. By the touch of an unselfish soul, even the regular sidewalk becomes holy.

I said in a previous work, heaven is where someone smiles because of you. And this is possible only when you reach out to another person in utter unselfishness, with the purest of desire to see that person happy. And this miraculous feat of humanity cannot be achieved by a sober, calculating person, it is only possible for a person crazy in love with society. So, be crazy, be mad, go absolutely bonkers, for the betterment of society, only then will the world witness the true dawn of sanity and sentience, through you - the miracle human.

The making of civilization is the work of a crazy lover, not a sober sleeper. Be a lover in front of whose radiant love, all theories, all philosophies, all words known to the intellectual world become dust - and all that remains is an eternal fragrance of sacrifice and salvation. What power does a paradigm hold in front of such love - what power does partisanism hold in front of such love - what power does nationality hold in front of such love! All things petty and barbarian get drowned in the gigantean rapids of such ever-effulgent love.

29. Lovenut Sonnet

Lovenut Sonnet

When I was a teenager,
There was a sticker on my desk.
My father had stuck it there,
Saying, till you reach your goal, don't rest.
Since that day I haven't stopped,
For I haven't reached my goal.
You may ask what the goal may be,
It is to die a lovenut lifting all.
Lovenut is one who is nuts,
Total bonkers for the benefit of society,
One whose lifeblood is sacrifice,
A revolutionary who is above all security.
I give a call to all the lovenuts of society.
Stop not till you remind all their humanity.

30. Life is Memory

Look at the mirror - what do you see - do you see yourself - puny and tiny, wrapped up in the traditional bounds of age-old tribalism - or do you see the world - the vast, eternal, uncontainable world - when you see the world in your own reflection, that's when a lover is born - that's when a torchbearer is born - that's when a human is born.

The cause is all-important - the cause of unity - the cause of universality. You are not alive till you are ready to die for the cause. What is death - it is nothing, it is merely the demise of the body - a body that holds no meaning whatsoever. It is the action committed by that body throughout its lifespan that counts.

And those who die for the cause, living every moment of their life realizing that cause, never ever die from the memories of time, though their bodies may perish. We are not bodies, but mere memories. So long as we live a life of deeds instead of pursuing recklessly the illusive phantom of pleasure, rest assured, our breath will never stop, instead will keep stirring up goodness in the hearts of humans long after we are gone.

Let me put it to you another way - after a brief few decades of life, if we exist at all, we all are going to live as memories - so the question is, are you going to exist as a memory of glory and pride or of disgust and dishonor. Life is either an instrument for memories of character, or nothing at all. And if someone says, they just don't care, then I have nothing to say to them, for as I said earlier, civilization is built by sleepless lovers, not careless sleepers.

31. Progress is Like Making Memory

The very fact that you are human, implies that you care, that you are accountable - and if you are not, then alas, bearing the title of human is not your cup of tea. But again, caring doesn't mean going bonkers with insecurity and fear of the unknown, caring simply means observing the world in its wholeness, as much as humanly possible, and then taking action to make sure that the society moves forward and not backward.

Society moves in whichever direction the mind moves. Whatever is in the mind, so is in society. If the mind is caring, the society is caring, if the mind is reckless and indifferent, the society is reckless and indifferent. The fate of the world depends on the tendencies of the mind.

Society is an extension of the mind, not the master. The only reason, society ends up as the master of the mind is because the mind of today thinks the societal extension of yesterday is their own. Hence they accept the rotten extension of their dead ancestors as the paradigm of their alive present. For the society to evolve, this very habit must be abolished.

Social development is quite like memory consolidation in the human brain. Important memories meticulously get imprinted from old dying neurons to newly born neurons and unimportant memories fade away while making way for new memories to flourish. Such should be the course of societal progress.

It is this simple, not everything that is old is bad, but at the same time, just because it is old and traditional, doesn't make it civilized. Accept whatever is wise and civilized from your past and discard everything that is out of place in a modern human society while enthusiastically exploring new uncharted territories of time and space.

BIBLIOGRAPHY

Archer M., (2000), Being Human: The Problem of Agency. Cambridge University Press.

Archer M., (2003), Structure, Agency and the Internal Conversation. Cambridge University Press.

Adolphs R (2003) Cognitive neuroscience of human social behaviour. Nature Rev Neurosci 4: 165–178.

Adolphs R, Tranel D, Damasio AR (2003) Dissociable neural systems for recognizing emotions. Brain Cogn 52: 61–69.

Afton, A. D. (1985). Forced copulation as a reproductive strategy of male lesser scaup: A field test of some predictions. - Behaviour 92, p. 146-167.

Allison T, Puce A, McCarthy G. (2000) Social perception from visual cues: role of the STS region. Trends Cogn Sci 4: 267–278.

Andresen, Jensine, and Robert Forman, eds. Cognitive Models and Spiritual Maps. Bowling Green, Ohio: Imprint Academic, 2000.

Ashbrook, James, and Carol Albright. The Humanizing Brain: Where Religion and Neuroscience Meet. Cleveland, OH: Pilgrim Press, 1997.

Azari, Nina, Janpeter Nickel, Gilbert Wunderlich, Michael Niedeggen, Harald Hefter, Lutz Tellmann, Hans Herzog, Petra Stoerig, Dieter Birnbacher, and Rudiger Seitz. "Neural Correlates of Religious Experience." European Journal of Neuroscience 13, no. 8 (2001)

Agar, N. (2004). Liberal eugenics: In defence of human enhancement. London: Blackwell Publishing.

Alteheld, N., Roessler, G., Vobig, M., & Walter, R. (2004). The retina implant new approach to a visual prosthesis. Biomedizinische Technik, 49(4), 99–103.

Antal, A., Nitsche, M. A., Kincses, T. Z., Kruse, W., Hoffmann, K. P., & Paulus, W. (2004a). Facilitation of visuo-motor learning by transcranial direct current stimulation of the motor and extrastriate visual areas in humans. European Journal of Neuroscience, 19(10), 2888–2892.

Bernstein R.J., (1971), Praxis and Action: Contemporary Philosophies of Human Activity. Philadelphia: University of Pennsylvania Press.

Bernstein R.J., (1976), The Restructuring Social and Political Thought.

Bernstein R.J., (1983), Beyond Relativism and Objectivism: Science, Hermeneutics, and Praxis. Philadelphia: University of Pennsylvania Press.

Bernstein R.J., (1986), Philosophical Profiles. Philadelphia: University of Pennsylvania Press.

Bernstein R.J., (1991), New Constellation. Cambridge: MIT Press.

Birkhead, T. R., Johnson, S. D. & Nettleship, D. N. (1985). Extra-pair matings and mate guarding in the common murre Uria aalge. - Anim. Behav. 33, p. 608-619.

Beauregard, Mario, and Vincent Paquette. "Neural Correlates of a Mystical Experience in Carmelite Nuns." Neuroscience Letters 405, no. 3 (2006)

Benson, Herbert. Timeless Healing: The Power and Biology of Belief. New York: Scribner, 1996

Bose, Subhas Chandra. An Indian Pilgrim: An Unfinished Autobiography, Oxford University Press, 1997

Bose, Subhas Chandra. The Indian Struggle 1920-1942, Oxford University Press, 1997

Bogen, J.E.(1995a), 'On the neurophysiology of consciousness: Part I. An overview', Consciousness and Cognition, 4.

Bogen, J.E. (1995b), 'On the neurophysiology of consciousness: Part II. Constraining the semantic problem', Consciousness and Cognition, 4.

Bremner, J. D., R. Soufer, et al. (2001). "Gender differences in cognitive and neural correlates of remembrance of emotional words." Psychopharmacol Bull 35 (3).

Brothers, L. (2002). The social brain: A project for integrating primate behavior and neurophysiology in a new domain. In J. T. Cacioppo et al. (Eds.), Foundations in neuroscience. Cambridge, MA: MIT Press.

Buss, D. D. (2003). Evolutionary Psychology: The New Science of Mind, 2nd ed. New York: Allyn & Bacon.

Buss, D. M. (1989). "Conflict between the sexes: Strategic interference and the evocation of anger and upset." J Pers Soc Psychol 56 (5).

Buss, D. M. (1995). "Psychological sex differences. Origins through sexual selection." Am Psychol 50 (3).

Buss, D. M. (2002). "Review: Human Mate Guarding." Neuro Endocrinol Lett 23 (Suppl 4).

Buss, D. M., and D. P. Schmitt (1993). "Sexual strategies theory: An evolutionary perspective on human mating." Psychol Rev 100 (2).

Blakemore SJ, Decety J (2001) From the perception of action to the understanding of intention. Nature Rev Neurosci 2: 561.

Bruce C, Desimone R, Gross CG (1981) Visual properties of neurons in a polysensory area in superior temporal sulcus of the macaque. J Neurophysiol 46: 369–384.

Buccino G, Vogt S, Ritzl A, Fink GR, Zilles K, Freund HJ, Rizzolatti G (2004) Neural circuits underlying imitation of hand actions: an event related fMRI study. Neuron 42: 323–34.

Colapietro V., (1988), "Human Agency: The Habits of Our Being." Southern Journal of Philosophy, XXVI, 2, pp. 153-68.

Colapietro V., (1992), "Purpose, Power, and Agency." The Monist, 75, 4 (October) pp. 423-44.

Colapietro V., (2004a), "C. S. Peirce's Reclamation of Teleology." Nature in American Philosophy, ed. Jean De Groot (Washington, D.C.: Catholic University Press of America), pp. 88-108.

Colapietro V., (2004b), "Portrait of a Historicist: An Alternative Reading of Peircean Semiotic." Semiotiche, 2/04 [maggio 2004], pp. 49-68.

Colapietro V., (2006), "Engaged Pluralism: Between Alterity and Sociality." The Pragmatic Century: Conversations with Richard J. Bernstein (Albany, NY: SUNY Press), pp. 39-68.

Carey DP, Perrett DI, Oram MW (1997) Recognizing, understanding and reproducing actions. In: Jeannerod M, Grafman J (eds) Handbook of neuropsychology. Vol. 11: Action and cognition. Elsevier, Amsterdam.

Carr L, Iacoboni M, Dubeau MC, Mazziotta JC, Lenzi GL (2003) Neural mechanisms of empathy in humans: a relay from neural systems for imitation to limbic areas. Proc Natl Acad Sci USA 100: 5497–5502.

Changeux JP, Ricoeur P (1998) La nature et la règle. Odile Jacob, Paris.

Chomsky Noam, (2017) Requiem for the American Dream

Chomsky Noam, (2016) Who Rules the World?

Chomsky Noam, (2010) How the World Works

Churchland, P.S. (1986), Neurophilosophy (Cambridge, MA: The MIT Press).

Churchland, P.S. & Ramachandran, V.S. (1993), 'Filling in: Why Dennett is wrong', in Dennett and His Critics: Demystifying Mind, ed. B. Dahlbom (Oxford: Blackwell Scientific Press).

Churchland, P.S., Ramachandran, V.S. & Sejnowski, T.J. (1994), 'A critique of pure vision', in Large- scale Neuronal Theories of the Brain, ed. C. Koch & J.L. Davis (Cambridge, MA: The MIT Press).

Crick, F. (1994), The Astonishing Hypothesis: The Scientific Search for the Soul (New York: Simon and Schuster).

Crick, F. (1996), 'Visual perception: rivalry and consciousness', Nature, 379.

Crick, F. & Koch, C. (1992), 'The problem of consciousness', Scientific American, 267.

Craig AD (2002) How do you feel? Interoception: the sense of the physiological condition of the body. Nature Rev Neurosci 3: 655–666.

Damasio, A (2003a) Looking for Spinoza. Harcourt Inc. Damasio A (2003b) Feeling of emotion and the self. Ann NY Acad Sci 1001: 253–261.

d'Aquili, Eugene. "Senses of Reality in Science and Religion." Zygon 17, no 4 (1982)

d'Aquili, Eugene. "The Biopsychological Determinants of Religious Ritual Behavior." Zygon 10, no. 1 (1975)

d'Aquili, Eugene. "The Myth-Ritual Complex: A Biogenetic Structural Analysis." Zygon 18, no. 3 (1983)

d'Aquili, Eugene, and Andrew Newberg. The Mystical Mind: Probing the Biology of Religious Experience. Minneapolis: Fortress Press, 1999.

Daly DD. 1958. Ictal affect. Am J Psychiatry.

Damasio, A. (1994) Descartes' Error: Emotion, Reason and the Human Brain. New York, Putnams.

Damasio, A. (1999) The Feeling of What Happens: Body, Emotion and the Making of Consciousness. London, Heinemann.

Darwin, C. (1859) On the Origin of Species by Means of Natural Selection. London, Murray.

Darwin, C. (1871) The Descent of Man and Selection in Relation to Sex. London, John Murray.

Darwin, C. (1872) The Expression of the Emotions in Man and Animals. London, John Murray; also published 1965, Chicago, University of Chicago Press.

Dawkins, M.S. (1987) Minding and mattering. In C. Blakemore and S. Greenfield (eds) Mindwaves. Oxford, Blackwell, 151-60.

Dawkins, R. (1976) The Selfish Gene. Oxford, Oxford University Press; a new edition, with additional material, was published in 1989.

Dawkins, R. (1986) The Blind Watchmaker. London, Longman.

Di Pellegrino G, Fadiga L, Fogassi L, Gallese V, Rizzolatti G (1992) Understanding motor events: A neurophysiological study. Exp Brain Res 91: 176–80.

Deikman, A.J. (2000) A functional approach to mysticism. Journal of Consciousness Studies 7(11-12), 75-91.

Delmonte, M.M. (1987) Personality and meditation. In M. West (ed.) The Psychology of Meditation. Oxford, Clarendon Press, 118-32.

Dennett, D.C. (1988) Quining qualia. In A.J. Marcel and E. Bisiach (eds) Consciousness in Contemporary Science. Oxford, Oxford University Press, 42-77.

Dennett, D.C. (1991) Consciousness Explained. Boston, MA, and London, Little, Brown and Co.

Dennett, D.C. (1995a) Darwin's Dangerous Idea. London, Penguin.

Dennett, D.C. (1995b) The unimagined preposterousness of zombies. Journal of Consciousness Studies 2(4), 322-6.

Dennett, D.C. (1995c) Cog: steps towards consciousness in robots. In T. Metzinger (ed.) Conscious Experience. Thorverton, Devon, Imprint Academic, 471-87.

Dennett, D.C. (1996a) Facing backwards on the problem of consciousness. Journal of Consciousness Studies 3(1), 4-6.

Dennett, D.C. (1996b) Kinds of Minds: Towards an Understanding of Consciousness. London, Weidenfeld & Nicolson.

Dennett, D.C. (1997) An exchange with Daniel Dennett. In J. Searle (ed.) The Mystery of Consciousness. New York, New York Review of Books, 115-19.

Dennett, D.C. (1998) The myth of double transduction. In S.R. Hameroff, A.W. Kaszniak and A. C. Scott (eds)

Toward a Science of Consciousness: The Second Tucson Discussions and Debates. Cambridge, MA, MIT Press, 97-107.

Dennett, D.C. (1998b) Brainchildren: Essays on Designing Minds. Cambridge, MA, MIT Press.

Dennett, D.C. (2001) The fantasy of first person science. Debate with D. Chalmers, Northwestern University, Evanston, IL, February 2001.

Dennett, D.C. (2003) Freedom Evolves. New York, Penguin.

Dennett, D.C. and Kinsbourne, M. (1992) Time and the observer: the where and when of consciousness in the brain. Behavioral and Brain Sciences 15, 183-247, including commentaries and authors' responses.

Dewey J., (1911 [1977]), "Epistemological Realism: The Alleged Ubiquity of the Knowledge Relation."

Journal of Philosophy, VIII, 20 (September 28, 1911).

Dewhurst, Kenneth, and A. W. Beard. "Sudden Religious Conversions in Temporal Lobe Epilepsy." British Journal of Psychiatry 117 (1970)

Dewhurst K, Beard AW. Sudden religious conversions in temporal lobe epilepsy. 1970 Epilepsy Behav 2003

Devinsky O, Lai G. Spirituality and religion in epilepsy. Epilepsy Behav 2008.

Devinsky, O., Morrell, MJ, Vogt, BA. (1995) 'Contribution of anterior cingulate cortex to behavior', Brain, 118.

Douglas Stone A., Chapter 24, The Indian Comet, in the book Einstein and the Quantum, Princeton University Press, Princeton, New Jersey, 2013.

E. Horvitz, "One Hundred Year Study on Artificial Intelligence: Reflections and Framing," ed: Stanford University, 2014.

Einstein A. (1925). "Quantentheorie des einatomigen idealen Gases". Sitzungsberichte der Preussischen Akademie der Wissenschaften.

Eckhart Meister, Selected Writings

Egidi R., ed. (1999), "Von Wright and 'Dante's Dream': Stages in a Philosophical Pilgrim's Progress", in In Search of a New Humanism: the Philosophy of G.H. von Wright, ed. by R. Egidi, Kluwer, Dordrecht.

Fadiga L, Fogassi L, Pavesi G, Rizzolatti G (1995) Motor facilitation during action observation: a magnetic stimulation study. J Neurophysiol 73: 2608–2611.

Fogassi L, Gallese V, Fadiga L, Rizzolatti G (1998) Neurons responding to the sight of goal directed hand/arm actions in the parietal area PF (7b) of the macaque monkey. Soc Neurosci Abs 24:257.5.

Frith U, Frith CD (2003) Development and neurophysiology of mentalizing. Philos Trans R Soc Lond B Biol Sci 358: 459.

Farah, M.J. (1989), 'The neural basis of mental imagery', Trends in Neurosciences, 10.

Finlay BL, Darlington RB (1995) Linked regularities in the development and evolution of mammalian brains. Science 268.

Freud, S. "The Interpretation of Dreams", 1900

Freud, S. "Selected papers on hysteria and other psychoneuroses" Journal of Nervous and Mental Disease 1909.

Freud, S. "The Origin and Development of Psychoanalysis", 1910

Freud, S. "Psychopathology of everyday life", 1914

Freud, S. "Beyond the Pleasure Principle", 1920

Frith, C.D. & Dolan, R.J. (1997), 'Abnormal beliefs: Delusions and memory', Paper presented at the May, 1997, Harvard Conference on Memory and Belief.

Gay, Volney, ed. Neuroscience and Religion. Plymouth, UK: Lexington Books, 2009.

Gazzaniga, M. S. (1985). The social brain. New York: Basic Books.

Gazzaniga, M.S. (1993), 'Brain mechanisms and conscious experience', Ciba Foundation Symposium, 174.

Geschwind N. "Behavioural changes in temporal lobe epilepsy". Psychol Med. 1979.

Gellhorn, E., Kiely, W.F. "Mystical states of consciousness: neurophysiological and clinical aspects." J Nerv Ment Dis. 1972;154:399-405.

Gilbert SL, Dobyns WB, Lahn BT (2005) Genetic links between brain development and brain evolution. Nat Rev Genet 6.

Gray JA. The Psychology of Fear and Stress. 2nd ed. New York, NY: Cambridge University Press; 1988.

Gloor, P. (1992), 'Amygdala and temporal lobe epilepsy', in The Amygdala: Neurobiological Aspects of Emotion, Memory and Mental Dysfunction, ed J.P. Aggleton (New York: Wiley-Liss).

Greenspan, S. I. and S. G. Shanker (2004). The first idea: How symbols, language, and intelligence evolved from our early primate ancestors to modern humans. Cambridge, MA: Da Capo Press.

Grady, D. (1993), 'The vision thing: Mainly in the brain', Discover, June.

Gallagher HL, Frith CD (2003) Functional imaging of 'theory of mind'. Trends Cogn Sci 7: 77.

Gallese V, Fogassi L, Fadiga L, Rizzolatti G (2002) Action representation and the inferior parietal lobule. In: Prinz W, Hommel B (eds) Attention & Performance XIX. Common mechanisms in perception and action. Oxford University Press, Oxford.

Gallese V, Keysers C, Rizzolatti G (2004) A unifying view of the basis of social cognition. Trends Cogn Sci 8: 396–403.

Gangitano M, Mottaghy FM, Pascual-Leone A (2001) Phase specific modulation of cortical motor output during movement observation. NeuroReport 12: 1489–1492.

Gangitano M, Mottaghy FM, Pascual-Leone A (2004) Modulation of premotor mirror neuron activity during observation of unpredictable grasping movements. Eur J Neurosci 20: 2193– 2202.

Goldman AI, Sripada CS (2004) Simulationist models of face-based emotion recognition. Cognition 94: 193–213.

Grèzes J, Costes N, Decety J (1998) Top-down effect of strategy on the perception of human biological motion: a PET investigation. Cogn Neuropsychol 15: 553–582.

Grèzes J, Armony JL, Rowe J, Passingham RE (2003) Activations related to "mirror" and "canonical" neurones in the human brain: an fMRI study. Neuroimage 18: 928–937.

Gross CG, Rocha-Miranda CE, Bender DB (1972) Visual properties of neurons in the inferotemporal cortex of the macaque. J Neurophysiol 35: 96–111.

Hari R, Forss N, Avikainen S, Kirveskari S, Salenius S, Rizzolatti G

(1998) Activation of human primary motor cortex during action observation: a neuromagnetic study. Proc. Natl Acad Sci USA 95: 15061–15065.

Hardy, G. H. (1940). Ramanujan. Cambridge: Cambridge University Press.

Hall, Daniel, Keith Meador, and Harold Koenig. "Measuring Religiousness in Health Research: Review and Critique." Journal of Religion and Health 47, no. 2 (2008)

Harris, Sam, Jonas Kaplan, Ashley Curiel, Susan Bookheimer, Marco Iacoboni, and Mark Cohen. "The Neural Correlates of Religious and Nonreligious Belief." PLoS One 4, no. 10 (October 1, 2009)

Halgren, E. (1992), 'Emotional neurophysiology of the amygdala within the context of human cognition', in The Amygdala:

Neurobiological Aspects of Emotion, Memory and Mental Dysfunction, ed J.P. Aggleton (New York: Wiley-Liss).

Halligan PW, Fink GR, Marshal JC, Vallar G. 2003. Spatial cognition: evidence from visual neglect. Trends Cogn Sci.

Handbook of Emotions, Edited by Michael Lewis, Jeannette M. Haviland-Jones, and Lisa Feldman Barrett, The Guilford Press; 3rd edition (2010).

Hameroff, S.R. and Penrose, R. (1996) Conscious events as orchestrated space-time selections. Journal of Consciousness Studies 3(1), 36-53; also reprinted in J. Shear (ed.) (1997) Explaining Consciousness-The Hard Problem. Cambridge, MA, MIT Press, 177-95.

Harding, D.E. (1961) On Having no Head: Zen and the Re-Discovery of the Obvious. London, Buddhist Society.

Hardy, A. (1979) The Spiritual Nature of Man: A Study of Contemporary Religious Experience. Oxford, Clarendon Press.

Harre, R. and Gillett, G. (1994) The Discursive Mind. Thousand Oaks, CA, Sage.

Haugeland, J. (ed.) (1997) Mind Design II: Philosophy, Psychology, Artificial Intelligence. Cambridge, MA, MIT Press.

Hauser, M.D. (2000) Wild Minds: What Animals Really Think. New York, Henry Holt and Co.; London, Penguin.

Hebb, D.O. (1949) The Organization of Behavior. New York, Wiley.

Helmholtz, H.L.F. von (1856-67) Treatise on Physiological Optics.

Hess, EH (1975) "The role of pupil size in communication," Scientific American, 233(5), 110–12.

Heyes, C.M. (1998) Theory of mind in nonhuman primates. Behavioral and Brain Sciences 21, 101-48; with commentaries.

Heyes, C.M. and Galef, B.G. (eds) (1996) Social Learning in Animals: The Roots of Culture. San Diego, CA, Academic Press.

Hilgard, E.R. (1986) Divided Consciousness: Multiple Controls in Human Thought and Action. New York, Wiley.

Hitler, Adolf. Mein Kampf, 1925

Hodgson, R. (1891) A case of double consciousness. Proceedings of the Society for Psychical Research 7, 221-58.

Hofstadter, D.R. and Dennett, D.C. (eds) (1981) The Mind's I: Fantasies and Reflections on Self and Soul. London, Penguin.

Holland, J. (ed.) (2001) Ecstasy: The Complete Guide: A Comprehensive Look at the Risks and Benefits of MDMA. Rochester, VT, Park Street Press.

Holmes, D.S. (1987) The influence of meditation versus rest on physiological arousal. In M. West (ed.) The Psychology of Meditation. Oxford, Clarendon Press, 81-103.

Holmstrom, David. 1992, Christian Science Monitor

Holt, J. (1999) Blindsight in debates about qualia. Journal of Consciousness Studies 6(5), 54-71.

Holloway RL (1996) Evolution of the human brain. In: Lock A, Peters CR (eds) Handbook of human symbolic evolution. Oxford University Press, Oxford

Iacoboni M, Woods RP, Brass M, Bekkering H, Mazziotta JC, Rizzolatti G (1999) Cortical mechanisms of human imitation. Science 286: 2526–2528.

Iacoboni M, Koski LM, Brass M, Bekkering H, Woods RP, Dubeau MC, Mazziotta JC, Rizzolatti G (2001) Reafferent copies of imitated actions in the right superior temporal cortex. Proc Natl Acad Sci USA 98: 13995–13999.

Jeannerod M (1988) The neural and behavioural organization of goal-directed movements. Clarendon Press, Oxford.

Johnson-Frey SH, Maloof FR, Newman-Norlund R, Farrer C, Inati S, Grafton ST (2003) Actions or hand-objects interactions? Human inferior frontal cortex and action observation. Neuron 39: 1053–1058.

Jackson, F. (1982) Epiphenomenal qualia. Philosophical Quarterly 32, 127-36.

James, W. (1890) The Principles of Psychology (2 volumes). London, Macmillan.

James, W. (1902) The Varieties of Religious Experience: A Study in Human Nature. New York and London, Longmans, Green and Co.

Jansen, K. (2001) Ketamine: Dreams and Realities. Sarasota, FL, Multidisciplinary Association for Psychedelic Studies.

Jay, M. (ed.) (1999) Artificial Paradises: A Drugs Reader. London, Penguin.

Jaynes, J. (1976) The Origin of Consciousness in the Breakdown of the Bicameral Mind. New York, Houghton Mifflin.

Johnson, M.K. and Raye, C.L. (1981) Reality monitoring. Psychological Review 88, 67-85.

Kadim I, Mahgoub O, Baqir S et al. (2015) Cultured meat from muscle stem cells: a review of challenges and prospects. J Integr Agr 14: 222–233

Kandel, E. R. In Search of Memory: The Emergence of a New Science of Mind, W. W. Norton & Company (2007).

Kandel E. R. Schwartz JH, Jessel TM. Principles of neural sciences. New York; McGraw Hill, 2000.

Kanwisher, N. (2001) Neural events and perceptual awareness. Cognition 79, 89-113; also reprinted inS. Dehaene (ed.) The Cognitive Neuroscience of Consciousness. Cambridge, MA, MIT Press, 89-113.

Karn, K. and Hayhoe, M. (2000) Memory representations guide targeting eye movements in a natural task. Visual Cognition 7, 673-703.

Kennedy, H., & Dehay, C. (1988). Functional implications of the anatomical organization of the callosal projections of visual areas V1 and V2 in the macaque monkey. Behav. Brain Res., 29, 225–236.

Kentridge, R.W. and Heywood, C.A. (1999) The status of blindsight. Journal of Consciousness Studies 6(5), 3-11.

Kihlstrom, J.F. (1996) Perception without awareness of what is perceived, learning without awareness of what is learned. In M. Velmans (ed.) The Science of Consciousness. London, Routledge, 23-46.

Kosslyn, S.M. (1980) Image and Mind. Cambridge, MA, Harvard University Press.

Kosslyn, S.M. (1988) Aspects of a cognitive neuroscience of mental imagery. Science 240, 1621-6.

Kinsbourne, M. (1995), 'The intralaminar thalamic nucleii', Consciousness and Cognition, 4.

Kjaer, Troels, Camilla Bertelsen, Paola Piccini, David Brooks, Jorgen Alving, and Hans Lou. "Increased Dopamine Tone during Meditation- Induced Change of Consciousness." Cognitive Brain Research 13, no. 2 (April 2002)

Kölmel HW. 1985. Complex visual hallucinations in the hemianopic field. J Neurol Neurosurg Psychiatry.

Koenig, Harold. "Research on Religion, Spirituality, and Mental Health: A Review." Canadian Journal of Psychiatry 54, no. 5 (May 2009)

Koenig, Harold, ed. Handbook of Religion and Mental Health. San Diego, CA: Academic Press, 1998

Kraepelin E. Psychiatry: A Textbook for Students and Physicians. New York, NY: Science History Publications; 1990.

Lauglin, Charles, John McManus, and Eugene d'Aquili. Brain, Symbol, and Experience. 2nd ed. New York: Columbia University Press, 1992

Lakoff, G. and M. Johnson (1999). Philosophy in the flesh. Basic Books: New York.

LeDoux, J. E. (1996). The emotional brain. New York: Simon & Schuster.

LeDoux, J.E. (1992), 'Emotion and the amygdala', in The Amygdala: Neurobiological Aspects of Emo- tion, Memory and Mental Dysfunction, ed J.P. Aggleton (New York: Wiley-Liss).

Levin, D.T. and Simons, D.J. (1997) Failure to detect changes to attended objects in motion pictures. Psychonomic Bulletin and Review 4, 501-6.

Levine,J. (1983) Materialism and qualia: the explanatory gap. Pacific Philosophical Quarterly 64, 354-61.

Levine,J. (2001) Purple Haze: The Puzzle of Consciousness. New York, Oxford University Press. Levine, S. (1979) A Gradual Awakening. New York, Doubleday.

Levinson, B.W. (1965) States of awareness during general anaesthesia. British Journal of Anaesthesia 37, 544-6.

Lewicki, P., Czyzewska, M. and Hoffman, H. (1987) Unconscious acquisition of complex procedural knowledge. Journal of Experimental Psychology: Learning, Memory and Cognition 13, 523-30.

Lewicki, P., Hill, T. and Bizot, E. (1988) Acquisition of procedural knowledge about a pattern of stimuli that cannot be articulated. Cognitive Psychology 20, 24-37.

Lewicki, P., Hill, T. and Czyzewska, M. (1992) Nonconscious acquisition of information. American Psychologist 47, 796-801.

Manthey S, Schubotz RI, von Cramon DY (2003). Premotor cortex in observing erroneous action: an fMRI study. Brain Res Cogn Brain Res 15: 296–307.

Mesulam MM, Mufson EJ (1982) Insula of the old world monkey. III: Efferent cortical output and comments on function. J Comp Neurol 212: 38–52.

Naskar, Abhijit. "Homo: A Brief History of Consciousness", 2015

Naskar, Abhijit. "What is Mind?", 2016

Naskar, Abhijit. "Love, God & Neurons: Memoir of A Scientist who found himself by getting lost", 2016

Naskar, Abhijit. "Principia Humanitas", 2017

Naskar, Abhijit. "We Are All Black: A Treatise on Racism", 2017

Naskar, Abhijit. "Either Civilized or Phobic: A Treatise on Homosexuality", 2017

Naskar, Abhijit. "I Am The Thread: My Mission", 2017

Naskar, Abhijit. "The Bengal Tigress: A Treatise on Gender Equality", 2017

Naskar, Abhijit. "Morality Absolute", 2017

Naskar, Abhijit. "Build Bridges not Walls: In the name of Americana", 2018

Naskar, Abhijit. "Fabric of Humanity", 2018

Naskar, Abhijit. "Lives To Serve Before I Sleep", 2019

Naskar, Abhijit. "Citizens of Peace: Beyond the Savagery of Sovereignty", 2019

Naskar, Abhijit. "The Constitution of The United Peoples of Earth", 2019

Naskar, Abhijit. "Neurons Giveth, Neurons Taketh Away | Abhijit Naskar | TEDxIIMRanchi", 2019 https://www.youtube.com/watch?v=B NX-Q0ySm80

Naskar, Abhijit. "Mission Reality", 2019

Naskar, Abhijit. "Operation Justice: To Make A Society That Needs No Law", 2019

Naskar, Abhijit. "Every Generation Needs Caretakers: The Gospel of Patriotism", 2020

Naskar, Abhijit. "Hurricane Humans: Give me accountability, I'll give you peace", 2020

Naskar, Abhijit. "Revolution Indomable", 2020

Naskar, Abhijit. "Servitude is Sanctitude", 2020

Naskar, Abhijit. "Good Scientist: When Science and Service Combine", 2020

Newberg, Andrew, and Jeremy Iversen. "The Neural Basis of the Complex Mental Task of Meditation: Neurotransmitter and Neurochemical

Considerations." Medical Hypotheses 61, no. 2 (2003).

Newberg, Andrew. "How God Changes Your Brain: An Introduction to Jewish Neurotheology", CCAR Journal: The Reform Jewish Quarterly, Winter 2016.

Newberg, Andrew, and Stephanie Newberg. "A Neuropsychological Perspective on Spiritual Development." In Handbook of Spiritual Development in Childhood and Adolescence, edited by Eugene Roehlkepartain, Pamela King, Linda Wagener, and Peter Benson. London: Sage Publications, Inc., 2005

Newberg, Andrew. "The Neurotheology Link An Intersection Between Spirituality and Health", Alternative and Complimentary Therapies, Vol 21 No 1, February 2015.

Newberg, Andrew, Nancy Wintering, Dharma Khalsa, Hannah

Roggenkamp, and Mark Waldman. "Meditation Effects on Cognitive Function and Cerebral Blood Flow in Subjects with Memory Loss: A Preliminary Study." Journal of Alzheimer's Disease 20, no. 2 (2010)

Nash, M. (1995), 'Glimpses of the mind', Time.

Nesse RM. Proximate and evolutionary studies of anxiety, stress and depression: synergy at the interface. Neurosci Biobehav Rev. 1999;23:895-903.

Nicolelis, Miguel. (2011) "Beyond Boundaries: The New Neuroscience of Connecting Brains with Machines--- and How It Will Change Our Lives", Times Books

O'Hara, K. and Scutt, T. (1996) There is no hard problem of consciousness. Journal of Consciousness Studies 3(4), 290-302, reprinted in J. Shear (ed.)

(1997) Explaining Consciousness. Cambridge, MA, MIT Press, 69-82.

O'Regan, J.K. (1992) Solving the "real" mysteries of visual perception: the world as an outside memory. Canadian Journal of Psychology 46, 461-88.

O'Regan, J.K. and Noe, A. (2001) A sensorimotor account of vision and visual consciousness. Behavioral and Brain Sciences 24(5), 883-917.

O'Regan, J.K., Rensink, R.A. and Clark,].]. (1999) Change-blindness as a result of "mudsplashes." Nature 398, 34.

Ornstein, R.E. (1977) The Psychology of Consciousness (2nd edn). New York, Harcourt.

Ornstein, R.E. (1986) The Psychology of Consciousness (3rd edn). New York, Pehguin.

Ornstein, R.E. (1992) The Evolution of Consciousness. New York, Touchstone.

Penfield W, Faulk ME (1955) The insula: further observations on its function. Brain 78: 445– 470.

Penrose, R. (1994), Shadows of the Mind (Oxford: Oxford University Press).

Penrose, R. (1989), The Emperor's New Mind: Concerning Computers, Minds and The Laws of Physics (Oxford: Oxford University Press).

Persinger, "'I would kill in God's name' role of sex, weekly church attendance, report of a religious experience and limbic lability" Perceptual and Motor Skills 1997.

Persinger "Experimental simulation of the God experience" Neurotheology 2003.

Persinger, M. A. (1993b). Personality changes following brain injury as a grief response to the loss of sense of self: Phenomenological themes as indices of local lability and neurocognitive restructuring as psycho- therapy. Psychological Reports, 72

Persinger, Corradini, Clement, Keaney, et al "Neurotheology and its convergence with neuroquantology" NeuroQuantology 2010.

Persinger, Koren and St-Pierre "The electromagnetic induction of mystical and altered states within the laboratory" Journal of Consciousness Exploration and Research 2010.

Persinger "Case report: A prototypical spontaneous 'sensed presence' of a sentient being and concomitant electroencephalographic activity in the clinical laboratory" Neurocase 2008.

Persinger and Saroka "Potential production of Hughlings Jackson's "parasitic consciousness" by physiologically-patterned weak transcerebral magnetic fields: QEEG and source localization" Epilepsy & Behavior 28 (2013).

Persinger. "The neuropsychiatry of paranormal experiences". J Neuropsychiatry Clin Neurosci 2001.

Persinger. "Neuropsychological bases of god beliefs", New York: Praeger, 1987

Persinger. "Temporal lobe epileptic signs and correlative behaviors displayed by normal populations", Journal of General Psychology, 1986

Perry BD, Pollard R. Homeostasis, stress, trauma, and adaptation. A neurodevelopmental view of childhood trauma. Child Adolesc Psychiatr Clin N Am. 1998;7:33.

Paré, D. & Llinás, R. (1995), 'Conscious and preconscious processes as seen from the standpoint of sleep-waking cycle neurophysiology', Neuropsychologia, 33.

Phillips ML, Young AW, Senior C, Brammer M, Andrew C, Calder AJ, Bullmore ET, Perrett DI, Rowland D, Williams SC, Gray JA, David AS (1997) A specific neural substrate for perceiving facial expressions of disgust. Nature 389: 495–498.

Phillips ML, Young AW, Scott SK, Calder AJ, Andrew C, Giampietro V, Williams SC, Bullmore ET, Brammer M, Gray JA (1998) Neural responses to facial and vocal expressions of fear and disgust. Proc R Soc Lond B Biol Sci 265: 1809–1817.

Puce A, Perrett D (2003) Electrophysiological and brain imaging of biological motion. Philosoph Trans Royal Soc Lond, Series B, 358: 435–445.

Ramachandran VS. Behavioral and magnetoencephalographic correlates of plasticity in the adult human brain. Proc Natl Acad Sci USA 1993; 90: 10413–20.

Ramachandran VS. Phantom limbs, neglect syndromes, repressed memories, and Freudian psychology. Int Rev Neurobiol 1994; 37: 291–333.

Ramachandran VS. Plasticity and functional recovery in neurology. Clin Med 2005; 5: 368–73.

Ramachandran VS, Hirstein W. The perception of phantom limbs. The D. O. Hebb lecture. Brain 1998; 121: 1603–30.

Ramachandran VS, Rogers-Ramachandran D, Cobb S. Touching the phantom limb. Nature 1995; 377: 489–90.

Ramachandran VS, Rogers-Ramachandran D. Phantom limbs and

neural plasticity. Arch Neurol 2000; 57: 317–20.

Ramachandran VS, Rogers-Ramachandran D. It's all done with mirrors. Sci Am Mind 2007; 18: 16–9.

Ramachandran VS, Rogers-Ramachandran D. Sensations referred to a patient's phantom arm from another subjects intact arm: perceptual correlates of mirror neurons. Med Hypotheses 2008; 70: 1233–4.

Ramachandran VS, Rogers-Ramachandran D, Stewart M. Perceptual correlates of massive cortical reorganization. Science 1992; 258: 1159–60.

Rizzolatti G, Craighero L (2004) The mirror-neuron system. Annu Rev Neurosci 27: 169–192.

Rizzolatti G, Fogassi L, Gallese V (2001) Neurophysiological mechanisms underlying the understanding and imitation of action. Nature Rev Neurosci 2:661–670.

Rock I, Victor J. Vision and touch: an experimentally created conflict between the two senses. Science 1964; 143: 594–6.

Rose´n B, Lundborg G. Training with a mirror in rehabilitation of the hand. Scand J Plast Reconstr Surg Hand Surg 2005; 39: 104–8.

Royet JP, Plailly J, Delon-Martin C, Kareken DA, Segebarth C (2003) fMRI of emotional responses to odors: influence of hedonic valence and judgment, handedness, and gender. Neuroimage 20: 713–728.

Rozin R Haidt J and McCauley CR (2000) Disgust. In: Lewis M, Haviland-Jones JM (eds) Handbook of Emotion. 2nd Edition. Guilford Press, New York, pp 637–653.

Saxe R, Carey S, Kanwisher N (2004) Understanding other minds: linking developmental psychology and functional neuroimaging. Annu Rev Psychol 55: 87–124.

S. J. Russell and P. Norvig, Artificial intelligence: a modern approach (3rd edition): Prentice Hall, 2009.

Singer T, Seymour B, O'Doherty J, Kaube H, Dolan RJ, Frith CD (2004) Empathy for pain involves the affective but not the sensory components of pain. Science 303: 1157–1162.

Smith A (1759) The theory of moral sentiments (ed. 1976). Clarendon Press, Oxford.

Sprengelmeyer R, Rausch M, Eysel UT, Przuntek H (1998) Neural structures associated with recognition of facial expressions of basic emotions Proc R Soc Lond B Biol Sci 265: 1927–1931.

Strafella AP, Paus T (2000) Modulation of cortical excitability during action observation: a transcranial magnetic stimulation study. NeuroReport 11: 2289–2292.

Schilling, Vincent. 2017, indian country today

Stein, Stephen K. 2017, The Sea in World History: Exploration, Travel, and Trade

Simonsen R (2015) Eating for the future: veganism and the challenge of in vitro meat. In: Stapleton P, Byers A (Hg). Biopolitics and utopia. Palgrave Macmillan, New York (2015), S 167–190

Tanaka K (1996) Inferotemporal cortex and object vision. Ann Rev Neurosci. 19: 109–140.

Tesla N. "My Inventions", 1919

T. R. Society, "Machine learning: the power and promise of computers that learn by example," ed. The Royal Society, 2017.

Tomasello M, Call J (1997) Primate cognition. Oxford University Press, Oxford.

Tremblay C, Robert M, Pascual-Leone A, Lepore F, Nguyen DK, Carmant L, Bouthillier A, Theoret H (2004) Action observation and execution: intracranial recordings in a human subject. Neurology. 63: 937–938.

Umilta MA, Kohler E, Gallese V, Fogassi L, Fadiga L, Keysers C, Rizzolatti G (2001) "I know what you are doing": a neurophysiological study. Neuron 32: 91–101.

195

MUCIZE INSAN

197

199